Table of contents

I. Introduction

Chapter 1: Overview of CBDC

CBDCs come in two forms: retail and wholesale. Retail CBDCs are designed for use by the general public and are meant to be used as a substitute for cash. They are typically used for everyday transactions and can be held in digital wallets. Wholesale CBDCs are meant for use by financial institutions and are used for large-value transactions between banks.

One of the main drivers of CBDC is the increasing demand for digital payments. The rise of digital payments has led to concerns about the future of cash, and CBDCs are seen as a potential solution to this issue. Additionally, CBDCs have the potential to offer several benefits over traditional payment systems[1], such as faster transaction speeds, lower costs, and increased financial inclusion.

Another driver of CBDC is the potential to improve the effectiveness of monetary policy. CBDCs could allow central banks to have more control over the money supply and could enable more precise implementation of monetary policy. This could potentially lead to more stable and predictable economic outcomes.

However, there are also several challenges associated with CBDCs. One of the biggest challenges is ensuring that CBDCs are secure and can withstand cyber attacks. Additionally, CBDCs raise concerns about privacy and data protection, as they could allow central banks to track and monitor transactions. There are also concerns about the potential impact of CBDCs on the financial system, particularly the potential for CBDCs to destabilize the banking system or disintermediate banks.

Despite these challenges, CBDCs are being explored by central banks around the world, with several countries already implementing or piloting CBDCs. The next chapters of this book will explore the advantages and disadvantages of CBDCs in more detail, as well as the challenges and opportunities associated with their implementation.

---

1 Payment systems refer to the set of processes, procedures, and technologies that enable the transfer of money between individuals, businesses, and other entities. These systems provide a way for buyers to pay for goods and services and for sellers to receive payment.

Chapter 2: Purpose of the Book

Overall, the purpose of this book is to provide a comprehensive and balanced analysis of CBDCs, examining both their potential benefits and risks. The book will serve as a valuable resource for anyone interested in understanding the potential of CBDCs and their potential role in the future of payments and the global financial system.

The book will explore the potential benefits of CBDCs, such as increased efficiency, lower transaction costs, and improved financial inclusion. It will also examine the challenges associated with CBDCs, such as operational and technical challenges, risks to financial stability, and privacy concerns.

In addition to examining the advantages and disadvantages of CBDCs, the book will also compare CBDCs with other payment systems, such as cash, traditional electronic payment systems, and cryptocurrencies[2]. This will help readers understand the unique characteristics of CBDCs and their potential role in the future of payments.

The book will also provide case studies of countries that have already implemented or are piloting CBDCs, such as China, Sweden, Uruguay, Bahamas, Nigeria, Jamaica, South Korea, and France. These case studies will help readers understand the practical challenges and opportunities associated with CBDC implementation.

Furthermore, the book will examine the regulatory issues and challenges associated with CBDCs, including legal and regulatory frameworks, cross-border transactions, and international cooperation and coordination.

Finally, the book will explore the potential future of CBDCs, including their potential impact on the global financial system, opportunities and challenges for emerging economies, and technological advancements and innovation.

---

2 Cryptocurrencies are digital or virtual currencies that use cryptography to secure and verify transactions and to control the creation of new units.

Chapter 3: Brief History of CBDC

The concept of Central Bank Digital Currency (CBDC) is relatively new, but it has its roots in the early days of digital payments. The first digital payments systems were introduced in the 1970s, with the introduction of electronic funds transfer (EFT) systems. These systems allowed banks to transfer funds electronically, without the need for physical checks or cash.

In the 1990s, the rise of the Internet and e-commerce led to the development of new payment systems, such as PayPal and other digital payment platforms. These platforms allowed individuals and businesses to make digital payments using their bank accounts or credit cards.

However, the introduction of digital payments raised concerns about the future of cash and the role of central banks in the digital economy. As a result, central banks around the world began exploring the concept of CBDCs.

The first country to seriously explore the concept of CBDCs was Ecuador, which began exploring the idea in 2014.

In 2015, the Bank of England released a research paper exploring the potential benefits and risks of CBDCs, and in 2016, the Bank of Canada began exploring the possibility of issuing a CBDC.

In 2017, the People's Bank of China (PBOC) announced that it was exploring the possibility of issuing a digital version of the yuan. This announcement sparked interest around the world, with many other central banks beginning to explore the concept of CBDCs.

In 2018, the Bank for International Settlements (BIS) released a report on CBDCs, which highlighted the potential benefits and risks of CBDCs and provided guidance for central banks exploring the concept.

In 2020, the Bahamas became the first country to fully implement a CBDC, with the introduction of the Sand Dollar.

II. What is CBDC?

Chapter 4: Definition of CBDC

Central Bank Digital Currency (CBDC) is a digital form of fiat[3] money that is issued and backed by a central bank. The central bank also ensures that the CBDCs maintain their value, just like traditional fiat currencies.

Unlike cryptocurrencies, CBDCs are not decentralized[4] and are controlled by the issuing central bank.

Unlike traditional currency, CBDC is digital and can be stored on electronic devices such as smartphones or computers.

CBDC is recognized as legal tender, meaning that it is accepted as a valid form of payment for all debts, public and private.

CBDC can be used as a tool for monetary policy, allowing central banks to more easily manage interest rates, inflation, and other economic indicators.

CBDCs are designed to be used as a form of payment, similar to cash or traditional electronic payments. They can be used to make purchases and payments, both online and in-person, and can be transferred between individuals or businesses.

---

3   Fiat money is a type of currency that has no intrinsic value and is not backed by a physical commodity such as gold or silver. Instead, it is declared legal tender by a government and is accepted as a medium of exchange based on the trust and confidence in the issuing authority. Fiat money is typically issued by central banks and is used as a means of exchange for goods and services within a country. The value of fiat money is determined by supply and demand and can be influenced by a range of economic and political factors such as inflation, interest rates, and government policies.

4   Decentralized refers to a system or network that operates without a central authority or control. Instead, decision-making power and control are distributed among all participants in the network, and transactions are verified and validated by a consensus mechanism that involves all parties.

Chapter 5: Types of CBDC

CBDC can be classified into different types, depending on their design and functionality:

- Retail CBDCs are designed to be used by the general public, similar to cash. They are issued by the central bank and can be held and used by individuals and businesses for daily transactions. Retail CBDCs can be either account-based or token-based.

- Wholesale CBDCs are designed for use by financial institutions, such as banks, for interbank transactions and settlements. They are issued by the central bank and can only be used by authorized financial institutions.

- Hybrid CBDCs combine features of both retail and wholesale CBDCs. They are designed to be used by both individuals and financial institutions for different types of transactions. Hybrid CBDCs can be either account-based or token-based.

- Synthetic CBDCs are not issued by the central bank but are instead created by a private entity or consortium, using a basket of assets as collateral. They are designed to be used as a stablecoin[5], with a value that is pegged to a fiat currency or a basket of currencies.

CBDC can also be classified based on their underlying technology:

- Blockchain[6]-based CBDCs use distributed ledger technology (DLT) to record and verify transactions

- Non-blockchain-based CBDCs use other types of technology, such as a centralized database or a hybrid model.

---

5 A stablecoin is a type of cryptocurrency that is designed to maintain a stable value relative to a particular asset, such as a fiat currency or a commodity. Stablecoins are typically backed by reserves of the underlying asset, which are held in a custodial account or on a blockchain. This backing helps to ensure the stability of the stablecoin's value, and provides investors with a reliable and predictable store of value.

There are different types of CBDCs, including:

- Account-based CBDCs - These are CBDCs that are linked to a specific account, such as a bank account. They can be transferred between accounts and used to make payments.

- Token-based CBDCs - These are CBDCs that are issued as digital tokens[7]. They can be transferred between individuals or businesses and used to make payments.

The design of CBDCs can also vary based on their privacy and security features. CBDCs can be anonymous, meaning that the identity of the user is not disclosed during a transaction, or traceable, meaning that the identity of the user can be traced through the transaction record. CBDCs can also be designed to have different levels of security, such as multi-factor authentication or biometric verification.

Overall, the type of CBDC that a central bank chooses to issue will depend on the specific needs and goals of their economy. The next chapters of this book will explore the potential benefits and risks of CBDCs in more detail, as well as the challenges and opportunities associated with their implementation.

---

6   Blockchain technology is a decentralized digital ledger that enables secure, transparent, and tamper-resistant storage and transfer of data. It consists of a network of interconnected computers (nodes) that collaborate to validate and record transactions and data entries in a time-stamped, unalterable, and immutable manner. Each block in the chain contains a hash of the previous block, creating a secure and transparent chain of blocks that provides a clear audit trail of all transactions. Blockchain technology is often associated with cryptocurrencies, but it has a wide range of potential applications in various industries, including finance, supply chain management, healthcare, and more.

7   Digital tokens are units of value that are created and managed using blockchain technology. They represent a wide range of assets, including virtual currencies, digital assets, and real-world assets. Digital tokens are created and issued through initial coin offerings (ICOs) or security token offerings (STOs), and can be bought, sold, and traded on cryptocurrency exchanges or used as a means of payment for goods and services.

Chapter 6: Characteristics of CBDC

CBDC has several unique characteristics that differentiate it from traditional forms of money:

- Digital: CBDC is a digital form of currency that is stored and transferred electronically, making it easier to use and more efficient than physical cash.

- Programmable: CBDC can be designed with programmable features, allowing for automated smart contracts[8] and other applications.

- Interoperable: CBDC can be interoperable with other payment systems and currencies, allowing for cross-border transactions and international payments.

- Traceable: CBDC can be designed to be traceable, allowing for greater transparency and accountability in financial transactions.

- Data privacy: CBDC can be designed with strong data privacy protections, ensuring that user data is kept confidential and secure.

- Secure: CBDC can be designed with robust security features, such as encryption, multi-factor authentication, and biometric verification.

---

8   Smart contracts are self-executing digital contracts that are programmed to automatically execute the terms of an agreement between two or more parties. They are powered by blockchain technology, which provides a secure and transparent way to store and verify the terms of the contract. Smart contracts can be used to automate a wide range of business processes, including financial transactions, legal agreements, and supply chain management.

III. Advantages of CBDC

Chapter 7: Lower Transaction Costs and Improved Efficiency

CBDC can be cheaper and more efficient than traditional money due to:

- Lower fees: CBDC can eliminate or reduce transaction fees associated with traditional payment methods, such as credit cards, wire transfers, and money orders. This can make payments more affordable, especially for small transactions.

- Faster settlement: CBDC can facilitate real-time settlement of payments, reducing the time and cost associated with clearing and settlement of transactions. This can also reduce the risk of fraud and error associated with delayed settlement.

- Lower infrastructure costs: CBDC can reduce the need for physical infrastructure, such as bank branches and ATMs, reducing the overhead costs associated with traditional banking services.

- Automated smart contracts: CBDC can be designed with programmable features, allowing for automated smart contracts and other applications. This can reduce the need for intermediaries, such as lawyers and brokers, reducing the cost of transactions.

- Reduced fraud: CBDC can be designed with strong security features, such as encryption and biometric verification, reducing the risk of fraud and cyber-attacks. This can reduce the cost associated with fraud detection and prevention.

- Improved record keeping: CBDC can improve record keeping and data management, making it easier to track and trace financial transactions. This can improve the efficiency of auditing, compliance, and regulatory processes.

- Reduced paperwork: CBDC can reduce the need for paperwork and physical documentation associated with traditional financial transactions, improving the efficiency of administrative processes.

Chapter 8: Increased financial inclusion

One of the primary advantages of CBDCs is their potential to increase financial inclusion. As mentioned earlier, millions of people around the world still lack access to formal financial services. CBDCs can help bridge this gap by providing a low-cost and accessible means of accessing financial services. With CBDCs, people would no longer need to rely on banks or other financial institutions to store and access their money, making financial services more accessible to a wider range of people.

In addition, CBDCs can be designed to be more inclusive and accessible to people who are traditionally excluded from the formal financial system. For example, CBDCs can be designed to be more user-friendly for people who are not familiar with traditional banking services, such as those in rural areas or low-income communities. CBDCs can also be designed to be more inclusive for people with disabilities, such as by incorporating accessibility features like text-to-speech or audio descriptions.

Moreover, CBDCs can help to promote financial stability and reduce the risk of financial crises. With traditional currency, banks and other financial institutions play a central role in the financial system, creating potential risks and vulnerabilities. CBDCs, on the other hand, can provide a more secure and stable form of currency that is directly backed by the central bank, reducing the risk of bank runs or other financial crises.

Finally, CBDCs can provide governments with greater visibility into the economy, allowing for more efficient and effective monetary policy. CBDCs can help central banks to better understand how money is being used, where it is being spent, and how it is flowing through the economy, allowing for more targeted and effective policy interventions.

Chapter 9: Reduced fraud and corruption

One of the primary advantages of CBDCs is their potential to reduce fraud and corruption. Traditional currency can be easily counterfeited, and transactions can be difficult to trace, making it an attractive target for criminals and fraudsters. CBDCs, on the other hand, are designed to be highly secure and difficult to counterfeit, making them less susceptible to fraud and corruption.

CBDCs can also be designed to be highly traceable, making it easier for law enforcement agencies to track and investigate suspicious transactions. By keeping a detailed record of all transactions on the blockchain, CBDCs can make it much more difficult for criminals to hide their activities, and can provide law enforcement with valuable evidence in cases of fraud, money laundering, and other financial crimes.

Moreover, CBDCs can be designed to incorporate advanced security features such as biometric authentication, which can significantly reduce the risk of identity theft and other types of fraud. Biometric authentication can help to ensure that only authorized individuals are able to access and use CBDCs, making it much more difficult for fraudsters to steal or misuse digital currency.

Another advantage of CBDCs is that they can help to reduce corruption by providing greater transparency and accountability in financial transactions. CBDCs can be designed to incorporate advanced auditing features, which can help to ensure that all transactions are properly recorded and accounted for. This can make it much more difficult for corrupt officials to siphon off public funds or engage in other types of financial misconduct.

Finally, CBDCs can help to promote financial inclusion and reduce the risk of financial exclusion. By providing a secure and accessible means of accessing financial services, CBDCs can help to bring more people into the formal financial system, reducing the risk of financial exclusion and the associated social and economic costs.

Chapter 10: Enhanced monetary policy

One of the primary advantages of CBDCs is their potential to enhance monetary policy. CBDCs can provide central banks with greater control over the money supply, making it easier for them to implement and manage monetary policy.

For example, central banks could use CBDCs to implement negative interest rates, which can help to stimulate economic growth by encouraging consumers and businesses to spend more money. Negative interest rates effectively charge consumers and businesses for holding money in savings accounts, incentivizing them to spend or invest their money instead. By implementing negative interest rates through CBDCs, central banks could more easily and effectively control the money supply and stimulate economic activity.

CBDCs can also provide central banks with greater flexibility in implementing monetary policy. Traditional monetary policy tools such as interest rate adjustments can take time to have an impact on the economy. CBDCs, on the other hand, can be designed to be more responsive and dynamic, allowing central banks to quickly adjust the money supply in response to changing economic conditions.

Moreover, CBDCs can help to reduce the risk of bank runs during times of financial crisis. In a traditional banking system, customers may withdraw their deposits en masse during times of economic uncertainty, leading to a liquidity crisis for the bank. CBDCs can provide a more stable and secure alternative, allowing consumers to store their money directly with the central bank, rather than relying on commercial banks.

Finally, CBDCs can help to reduce the risk of currency fluctuations and exchange rate volatility. By providing a stable and secure form of digital currency, CBDCs can help to reduce the risk of currency fluctuations and provide greater financial stability. This can be particularly important for countries with volatile currencies or unstable financial systems.

IV. Disadvantages of CBDC

Chapter 11: Threat to commercial banks

While CBDCs offers many potential benefits over traditional currency, it also poses some potential drawbacks. One significant concern is that the widespread adoption of CBDCs could pose a threat to the existence of commercial banks, as it could reduce the demand for traditional banking services.

CBDCs are designed to be highly secure and easy to use, making them an attractive alternative to traditional banking services. Consumers could store their money directly with the central bank, rather than relying on commercial banks to store their deposits. This could lead to a significant decline in demand for commercial banking services, as consumers and businesses increasingly turn to CBDCs as a more secure and reliable form of digital currency.

This could pose a significant threat to the viability of commercial banks, as they rely on customer deposits to fund their lending activities. If customers begin to withdraw their deposits en masse and store them in CBDCs, it could lead to a significant reduction in the amount of money available for commercial banks to lend out. This could, in turn, lead to a contraction in lending activity, which could have negative implications for economic growth.

Furthermore, CBDCs could also pose a threat to the payment processing industry. As CBDCs are designed to be highly efficient and cost-effective, they could potentially replace traditional payment processing systems, such as credit card networks, wire transfer services, and other payment processors. This could have negative implications for the companies that provide these services, as they would no longer be needed in a world where CBDCs are the primary form of digital currency.

Chapter 12: Privacy concerns

One of the major concerns associated with the implementation of CBDC is privacy. CBDCs are digital currencies that can be easily tracked and traced by central authorities, potentially giving governments unprecedented access to financial data. While this increased monitoring could have some benefits, it also raises significant concerns about privacy and civil liberties.

CBDCs are designed to be highly secure and efficient, which means that every transaction is recorded on a central ledger, making it easier for governments to track financial activity. While this could be beneficial in preventing fraud and money laundering, it also means that the government would have access to detailed information about every transaction that takes place. This level of surveillance could be concerning for individuals who value their privacy and do not want their financial activity to be monitored by the government.

Moreover, governments could use CBDCs to impose greater control over financial transactions. For example, governments could set limits on the amount of money that individuals or businesses can hold, or even block transactions deemed to be illegal or undesirable. This could potentially infringe on individual freedoms and limit financial flexibility.

Another issue is that the implementation of CBDCs could make it easier for cybercriminals to gain access to sensitive financial data. If the central ledger is not secure, hackers could potentially gain access to sensitive financial data, putting individuals and businesses at risk of financial fraud and identity theft.

Furthermore, CBDCs could exacerbate financial inequality. People who do not have access to digital devices or reliable internet connections would be unable to participate in the digital economy, further marginalizing those who are already economically disadvantaged.

Chapter 13: Operational and technical challenges

While CBDC offers many potential benefits over traditional currency, it also poses several operational and technical challenges. Implementing a CBDC requires a significant investment in infrastructure and technology, as well as careful consideration of various operational factors.

One of the significant challenges of CBDC implementation is the creation and maintenance of a secure and reliable digital infrastructure. The digital infrastructure needs to be designed in a way that ensures the secure storage and transfer of funds, while also being able to handle large transaction volumes efficiently.

Another challenge is the integration of CBDC with existing payment systems. The implementation of CBDCs would require significant changes to payment systems to accommodate the new currency, which could lead to technical difficulties and operational inefficiencies. The interoperability of CBDC with existing payment systems must be ensured to ensure smooth and seamless transactions.

Moreover, CBDC implementation requires a significant investment in the development of regulatory frameworks and legal frameworks. There must be clear rules and regulations that govern the use of CBDCs, ensuring they are used for legitimate purposes and do not promote illicit activities such as money laundering or terrorism financing. Clear legal frameworks would also provide a legal basis for dispute resolution, fraud prevention, and compensation for losses.

Finally, the implementation of CBDCs requires public trust and confidence. For CBDCs to be widely adopted, the public must have confidence in their safety, reliability, and ease of use. The public must also trust that the central bank will safeguard their funds and prevent any misuse of their financial data.

Chapter 14: Implementation and adoption issues

One of the significant challenges of CBDC implementation is the coordination and collaboration among various stakeholders. The implementation of CBDCs requires the involvement of several stakeholders, including central banks, commercial banks, payment service providers, regulatory bodies, and other financial institutions. Ensuring effective coordination and collaboration among these stakeholders is essential to ensure the successful implementation of CBDCs.

Another challenge is the standardization of CBDCs. The standardization of CBDCs is critical to ensure their interoperability and compatibility with existing payment systems. Standardization would also help facilitate cross-border transactions and improve overall efficiency. However, achieving a consensus on standards and protocols could be challenging, as different jurisdictions may have different requirements and preferences.

Moreover, the adoption of CBDCs by the public and businesses is another significant challenge. The success of CBDCs relies on their widespread adoption by the public and businesses. However, achieving widespread adoption may be difficult, especially in regions where the use of cash is still prevalent. Additionally, many people may be hesitant to adopt new technologies, especially when it comes to financial transactions.

Another challenge is the integration of CBDCs with other payment systems. CBDCs must be integrated with existing payment systems, including digital wallets and mobile payment platforms. This integration requires significant investment in infrastructure and technology, as well as close collaboration with payment service providers and other financial institutions.

Finally, the implementation of CBDCs could have a significant impact on the financial sector, including commercial banks and other financial institutions. CBDCs could threaten the business models of commercial banks by reducing their role in the payment system and increasing competition. This could result in job losses and significant disruptions to the financial sector.

Chapter 15: Risks of centralization

One of the potential disadvantages of CBDC is the risk of centralization. CBDCs are designed to be issued and controlled by central banks, which may give them significant control over the financial system. While centralization may have some advantages, it also poses several risks that policymakers must consider when designing and implementing CBDCs.

One of the primary risks of centralization is the potential for abuse of power. Central banks may use their control over CBDCs to influence or manipulate the economy or financial markets. For example, they could use CBDCs to artificially inflate or deflate the value of the currency, which could have significant negative impacts on businesses and individuals.

Another risk is the potential for data breaches or cyber-attacks. CBDCs are digital currencies that are stored in centralized databases. This centralized storage creates a single point of failure that could be targeted by cybercriminals. A successful attack could result in the loss of significant amounts of wealth and could have severe economic consequences.

Centralization also creates a risk of discrimination. Central banks may use CBDCs to monitor and control transactions, which could lead to discrimination against certain individuals or groups. For example, central banks could use CBDCs to track the spending habits of individuals or to deny transactions to individuals based on their creditworthiness or other factors.

Moreover, centralization could create a risk of systemic failure. Central banks are responsible for maintaining the stability of the financial system. However, the centralized control of CBDCs may increase the risk of systemic failure in the event of a crisis. If the centralized system were to fail, it could have significant negative impacts on the economy and financial system.

V. Comparison of CBDC with other payment systems

Chapter 16: Cash

Chapter 17: Traditional electronic payment systems

Chapter 18: Cryptocurrencies

Chapter 16: Cash

Cash has been the traditional means of payment for centuries. It is widely accepted, easily transferable, and does not require any technical infrastructure. However, with the rise of digital payments, the use of cash is declining.

One of the main advantages of cash is that it is anonymous. Transactions made with cash are not recorded, and the identity of the payer is not disclosed. This anonymity provides a degree of privacy, which is important for some users. In contrast, CBDCs are likely to be fully traceable, and the identity of the payer will be known. This lack of privacy could be a disadvantage for some users who value their privacy.

Another advantage of cash is that it is widely accepted. It is accepted by almost all merchants and is used for everyday transactions. CBDCs are still in the development phase and may take some time before they are widely accepted.

Cash is also a reliable means of payment. It does not depend on the availability of technical infrastructure, and there is no risk of technical failure. In contrast, CBDCs rely on technical infrastructure, and there is a risk of technical failure or cyber-attacks, which could disrupt the payment system.

Another advantage of cash is that it does not require a bank account. Anyone can use cash, regardless of whether they have a bank account or not. In contrast, CBDCs are likely to be linked to a bank account or some form of digital wallet, which may exclude people who do not have access to these services.

Finally, cash provides a degree of financial independence. It is not controlled by any central authority and can be used without any restrictions. In contrast, CBDCs are likely to be issued and controlled by central banks, which may impose restrictions on their use.

Chapter 17: Traditional electronic payment systems

Traditional electronic payment systems such as credit and debit cards, bank transfers, and e-wallets have been widely used for several years. These payment systems have become more sophisticated with the development of technology, and they offer several advantages over cash.

One of the main advantages of traditional electronic payment systems is their convenience. They allow users to make payments quickly and easily, without the need for physical cash. In contrast, CBDCs may require additional technical infrastructure, such as digital wallets or mobile apps, which could limit their convenience.

Another advantage of traditional electronic payment systems is their interoperability. They can be used to make payments across borders and between different payment systems, which makes them a useful tool for international trade and commerce. In contrast, CBDCs are likely to be issued and controlled by individual central banks, which may limit their interoperability.

Traditional electronic payment systems are also widely accepted by merchants and are a standard part of the payment infrastructure. This widespread acceptance means that users do not need to worry about whether a particular merchant accepts a particular payment system. In contrast, CBDCs may take some time before they are widely accepted and may require additional technical infrastructure.

Finally, traditional electronic payment systems are familiar to users, and they have been used for several years. This familiarity means that users are more likely to trust these payment systems and use them with confidence. In contrast, CBDCs are a relatively new concept, and users may be hesitant to use them until they become more familiar with them.

Chapter 18: Cryptocurrencies

One of the main advantages of cryptocurrencies is their decentralization. They are not controlled by any central authority, such as a government or a central bank, which makes them immune to government or bank intervention.

Cryptocurrencies also offer anonymity and privacy to users. Transactions are recorded on a public ledger, but the identity of the parties involved in the transaction is not revealed. This anonymity makes cryptocurrencies a popular choice for those who value their privacy. In contrast, CBDCs may be subject to stricter regulations and may not offer the same level of anonymity.

Another advantage of cryptocurrencies is their global reach. They can be used to make payments across borders without the need for currency exchange or the involvement of intermediaries. In contrast, CBDCs may be limited to a specific jurisdiction or currency area.

Cryptocurrencies also offer a high degree of security. They use advanced cryptography to protect transactions from fraud and theft, and their decentralized nature makes them difficult to hack or manipulate.

However, cryptocurrencies also have several disadvantages. They are subject to high volatility, which makes them a risky investment option. Their anonymity also makes them attractive to criminal activities, such as money laundering and terrorism financing.

Furthermore, their lack of regulation and legal framework may limit their acceptance by merchants and financial institutions.

In contrast, CBDCs are likely to be subject to stricter regulations and may offer a higher level of security and stability. They may also be more widely accepted by merchants and financial institutions due to their central bank backing and legal framework.

VI. Case studies of CBDC implementation

Chapter 19: China

China has been one of the pioneers in developing and implementing a Central Bank Digital Currency (CBDC), called the Digital Currency Electronic Payment (DCEP). The DCEP pilot program was launched in 2020, and since then, it has been gradually expanded to cover more regions in the country.

The DCEP is designed to function as a digital version of the Chinese yuan (e-CNY), and it aims to facilitate peer-to-peer transactions and reduce reliance on cash and other forms of physical currency.

In 2021 tens of thousands of stores and businesses accept e-CNY. Long-distance transfers are being tested. ATM machines in China can accept foreign currencies and convert them into digital yuan, instantly issuing a plastic card and electronic account to use it.

At the beginning of 2022, 140 million users have opened wallets with e-CNY and made $10 billion in transactions. 10 million corporate accounts have been opened. 1.5 million entrepreneurs are ready to accept payments in digital yuan.

Trials of the e-CNY in the first half of 2022, for example as a means of payment during the Beijing Olympics, were impressively successful.

As of 2023, the DCEP has been rolled out to a large extent, with reports suggesting that it is being widely used by Chinese citizens for various types of transactions.

The official launch date has not yet been announced as such, so the Chinese CBDC (DCEP) is still in a pilot version.

However, 31 provinces/autonomous regions are using the digital yuan. 5 million entrepreneurs accept it as a means of payment. Consumers have made 260 million transactions.

Chapter 20: Sweden

Sweden is one of the countries with the lowest use of cash in the world, which made it easier for the country to develop an e-krona. The Swedish Riksbank is implementing a digital currency pilot project from February 2020 to February 2021.

The Swedish central bank, Riksbank, has been exploring the possibility of issuing an e-krona, a digital version of the country's currency. In 2017, Riksbank launched a pilot program to test the feasibility of an e-krona, and in 2020, the bank released a report on the potential implementation of an e-krona.

The Riksbank's next phase of the e-krona project in 2023 will involve several activities, including:

- Investigating the impact of an e-krona on the Swedish economy.

- Conducting testing of the technical infrastructure for the e-krona, with a focus on offline payments and sustainability.

- Examining whether and how the introduction of an e-krona would affect the Riksbank's existing mandate and determining the necessary legal amendments required for the Riksbank to issue an e-krona.

- Engaging in a dialogue with various stakeholders, such as other authorities and the market, through the external dialogue forum that was established in 2022.

- Carrying out user studies aimed at both end-users and traders.

- Preparing for the potential procurement of an issuable e-krona.

Chapter 21: Bahamas

The Bahamas is a small island nation in the Caribbean that has recently implemented a CBDC called the Sand Dollar. The Sand Dollar is pegged to the Bahamian dollar, which is in turn pegged to the US dollar, and is **the first CBDC to be launched in the world**.

The Sand Dollar was launched in October 2020 and is designed to provide a secure and efficient payment system that is accessible to all members of society. The Central Bank of the Bahamas (CBOB) has emphasized that the Sand Dollar is not intended to replace cash but rather to complement it, offering a digital payment option that is secure and convenient.

One of the main reasons for the implementation of the Sand Dollar is to increase financial inclusion. The Bahamas is a country with a high level of cash usage, and many members of society do not have access to traditional banking services. The Sand Dollar is designed to provide a secure and efficient payment system that is accessible to all members of society, including those who are underserved by traditional financial institutions.

Another reason for the implementation of the Sand Dollar is to reduce the costs and risks associated with cash transactions. The CBOB estimates that cash transactions cost the country around $60 million annually in handling, storage, and security costs. The Sand Dollar is designed to reduce these costs and provide a more efficient payment system for the country.

The implementation of the Sand Dollar has not been without its challenges. The CBOB has had to address concerns about user privacy and security, as well as concerns about the impact on the traditional banking sector. The CBOB has emphasized that the Sand Dollar is designed to complement traditional banking services and that it is not intended to replace them.

Overall, the implementation of the Sand Dollar in the Bahamas is an important milestone in the development of CBDCs.

Chapter 22: Nigeria

Nigeria is a large country in West Africa with a population of over 200 million people. Nigeria has a high level of cash usage. In February 2021, The Central Bank of Nigeria (CBN) launched the acclaimed eNaira, the first CBDC on the African continent.

Although eNaira is a pilot, it is completely open to the public, although initially it was only available to bank account holders. Only 80 vendors are currently active, according to Nigerian BusinessDay, citing a lack of demand.

As for the results of the implementation, there is not enough information available for the year 2022. However, according to the Governor of the Central Bank of Nigeria, the eNaira was designed to help reduce the cost of cash management, improve financial inclusion, and make cross-border transactions more efficient and secure.

It is worth noting that the implementation of the eNaira faced some initial challenges, including difficulties in registering for the digital currency and long wait times for transactions to be confirmed.

Although the eNaira app has been downloaded 764,000 times, almost half of them have never used it. The central bank has registered less than a third of the loaded number and 168,300 accounts are active. However, only 18,460 topped up wallets, including 80 merchants.

Only 1 in 200 Nigerians use eNaira, according to Bloomberg. And this after the government introduced rebates and other incentives as a desperate measure to draw attention to the digital currency.

Nigerians prefer to use stablecoin Tether (USDT).

Chapter 23: Jamaica

Jamaica is a small island nation in the Caribbean with a population of approximately 2.9 million people. In August 2020, The Bank of Jamaica (BOJ) announced that it had partnered with global technology firm Ecurrency Mint Limited to begin testing a CBDC.

The Bank of Jamaica (BOJ) successfully completed a pilot of their Central Bank Digital Currency (CBDC) with vendor eCurrency Mint Inc. in their Fintech Regulatory Sandbox in March 2021. BOJ had issued an Expression of Interest in July 2020 inviting technology providers to submit proposals to support testing a CBDC solution in their Fintech Regulatory Sandbox. BOJ partnered with eCurrency to enable the issuance and distribution of CBDC in a public-private partnership in Jamaica. The eCurrency solution allows the central bank to issue legal tender as a bearer instrument in digital form, using the Jamaican dollar (JMD).

Minister of Finance and the Public Service Dr. Nigel Clarke announced that the BOJ's CBDC, named JAM-DEX, would be rolled out by early 2022. The BOJ will preserve its role as the sole issuer of the national currency while empowering regulated financial institutions, including commercial banks and payment service providers, to use the CBDC.

No specific information was found on the results of Jamaica's CBDC implementation. However, a survey conducted in 2021 revealed that 85% of central banks surveyed were exploring the benefits and drawbacks of CBDCs, indicating a growing interest in implementing CBDCs in many countries. Additionally, the implementation of CBDCs involves a complex balance of cooperation and competition between the central bank and private payment service providers.

Overall, the available web search results suggest that Jamaica's CBDC implementation is progressing well and has generated interest in other countries, but specific information on the results of the implementation is not readily available.

Chapter 24: France

France has been actively working on the implementation of Central Bank Digital Currency (CBDC) for quite some time now, with the Banque de France spearheading the efforts. Here is a summary of the information available on the implementation of CBDC in France and the results of this implementation as of March 2023:

Implementation of CBDC in France:

- The Banque de France launched a wholesale CBDC program in March 2020, with a focus on experimenting with a digital euro for wholesale purposes.

- The Banque de France successfully conducted a CBDC experiment with a group of economic players, driven by Euroclear, in June 2021. The experiment consisted of simulating the issuance and subscription of government bonds on a permissioned blockchain using a CBDC.

- The Banque de France has completed the first phase of its wholesale CBDC program and published a report on the results in November 2021. The report highlights the benefits and drawbacks of CBDC and provides insights on its potential use cases.

Results of CBDC Implementation in France as of March 2023:

- The Banque de France aims to have a working wholesale CBDC ready by 2023 and has been stepping up its efforts in this regard.

- The Banque de France has successfully tested the use of CBDC for settling digital bonds by the European Investment Bank on a blockchain, with investors subscribing to EIB-issued digital bonds for a total amount of 100 million euros.

- However, it is not clear yet what the full impact of CBDC implementation in France will be in 2023, as the Banque de France is still in the experimental phase and the implementation of CBDC is a complex process that requires careful consideration of various factors.

In summary, France has been actively working on the implementation of CBDC, with the Banque de France leading the efforts. While the Banque de France aims to have a working wholesale CBDC ready by 2023, it is not yet clear what the full impact of CBDC implementation in France will be in 2023.

VII. Regulatory issues and challenges

Chapter 25: Legal and regulatory frameworks

Chapter 26: Cross-border transactions and interoperability

Chapter 27: International cooperation and coordination

Chapter 25: Legal and regulatory frameworks

One of the main regulatory issues and challenges associated with the implementation of CBDC is the legal and regulatory framework surrounding its use. Unlike traditional currency, which is backed by a central bank and subject to established legal and regulatory frameworks, CBDCs are a relatively new and untested form of currency that require a unique set of regulations and laws.

One of the main challenges in this regard is determining the legal status of CBDCs. Currently, most legal systems do not recognize digital currencies as legal tender, and as such, there is a lack of legal clarity surrounding the use and regulation of CBDCs. This can make it difficult for businesses and individuals to understand their rights and obligations when using CBDCs.

Another regulatory issue related to CBDCs is ensuring that they comply with existing laws and regulations, such as those related to anti-money laundering (AML) and know-your-customer (KYC) requirements. Because CBDCs are a relatively new form of currency, there may be gaps in existing AML/KYC regulations that need to be addressed to ensure that CBDCs are not used for illicit activities such as money laundering and terrorism financing.

In addition, the regulatory framework surrounding CBDCs needs to ensure that they are interoperable with existing payment systems, both domestically and internationally. This will require coordination and cooperation between central banks, financial institutions, and regulatory bodies to establish common standards and protocols for the use and exchange of CBDCs.

Finally, regulatory frameworks must also take into account the privacy concerns associated with the use of CBDCs. As discussed earlier, CBDCs have the potential to provide increased financial privacy to users, but there is also a risk that they could be used for illicit activities. As such, regulatory frameworks must strike a balance between ensuring that CBDCs are used for legitimate purposes while protecting the privacy rights of users.

Chapter 26: Cross-border transactions and interoperability

Cross-border transactions and interoperability are another set of regulatory issues and challenges associated with the implementation of Central Bank Digital Currencies (CBDCs). CBDCs have the potential to facilitate cross-border transactions, but this requires coordination and cooperation between central banks and regulatory bodies across different jurisdictions.

One of the key challenges in this regard is ensuring interoperability between different CBDC systems. Interoperability refers to the ability of different CBDC systems to work together seamlessly, allowing users to transact across different systems. This requires the establishment of common standards and protocols for the use and exchange of CBDCs, as well as coordination between central banks and regulatory bodies in different jurisdictions.

In addition, cross-border transactions involving CBDCs raise a number of regulatory issues related to anti-money laundering (AML) and know-your-customer (KYC) requirements.

Another regulatory issue related to cross-border transactions and interoperability is the need to establish mechanisms for resolving disputes and enforcing legal agreements between parties in different jurisdictions. This requires coordination and cooperation between legal systems and regulatory bodies in different jurisdictions to ensure that disputes can be resolved efficiently and effectively.

Finally, regulatory frameworks must also take into account the potential impact of CBDCs on the stability of the global financial system. Because CBDCs have the potential to disrupt existing financial systems and create new forms of competition, there is a need to ensure that CBDCs are integrated into the existing financial system in a way that supports financial stability and prevents systemic risks.

Chapter 27: International cooperation and coordination

International cooperation and coordination are critical regulatory issues and challenges associated with the implementation of Central Bank Digital Currencies (CBDCs). Because CBDCs have the potential to impact the global financial system and cross-border transactions, coordination and cooperation between central banks and regulatory bodies in different jurisdictions are essential.

One of the key challenges in this regard is the need to establish common standards and protocols for the use and exchange of CBDCs across different jurisdictions. This requires coordination and cooperation between central banks, financial institutions, and regulatory bodies in different countries to ensure that CBDCs can be used seamlessly and securely across borders.

Because CBDCs have the potential to disrupt existing financial systems and create new forms of competition, there is a need for international cooperation and coordination to ensure that CBDCs are integrated into the existing financial system in a way that supports financial stability and prevents systemic risks.

In addition, international cooperation and coordination are important for addressing regulatory issues related to anti-money laundering (AML) and know-your-customer (KYC) requirements. Because CBDCs are a relatively new form of currency, there may be gaps in existing AML/KYC regulations that need to be addressed to ensure that CBDCs are not used for illicit activities such as money laundering and terrorism financing. International cooperation and coordination can help to establish common standards and best practices for AML/KYC regulations related to CBDCs.

Finally, international cooperation and coordination are also important for addressing issues related to data privacy and security. Because CBDCs involve the use of digital technologies and the exchange of sensitive financial data, there is a need for international standards and protocols to ensure that CBDCs are secure and protect the privacy of users.

VIII. Future of CBDC

Chapter 28: Potential impact on the global financial system

The future of Central Bank Digital Currencies (CBDCs) is a topic of much debate and speculation. While CBDCs have the potential to transform the global financial system, there are also concerns about their potential impact on financial stability and the privacy of users.

One potential impact of CBDCs on the global financial system is the potential for increased financial inclusion. CBDCs have the potential to provide access to financial services to people who are currently unbanked or underbanked, which could help to reduce poverty and promote economic growth.

Because CBDCs are digital and can be exchanged without the need for intermediaries, they could help to reduce transaction costs and increase the speed of transactions, which could benefit businesses and consumers alike.

However, there are also concerns about the potential risks associated with CBDCs. One concern is the potential for increased financial instability if CBDCs were to replace cash and bank deposits as a store of value. This could lead to a decrease in the demand for bank deposits, which could in turn reduce the amount of funding available for banks to lend, potentially leading to a credit crunch and financial instability.

Another concern is the potential impact of CBDCs on monetary policy. CBDCs could potentially make it more difficult for central banks to implement monetary policy, as they could undermine the effectiveness of traditional monetary policy tools such as interest rate adjustments.

Privacy is another key concern related to the future of CBDCs. While CBDCs have the potential to provide greater privacy and security compared to traditional payment methods, there are also concerns about the potential for governments and central banks to monitor and track the use of CBDCs, potentially infringing on users' privacy rights.

Chapter 29: Opportunities and challenges for emerging economies

As Central Bank Digital Currencies (CBDCs) become more widely adopted, emerging economies may have both opportunities and challenges to consider. Here are some of the potential impacts of CBDCs on these economies.

Opportunities:

- Increased Financial Inclusion: CBDCs can help improve financial inclusion in emerging economies by providing a low-cost alternative to traditional banking systems. They can also help reach underbanked or unbanked populations by offering digital payment solutions without requiring access to a traditional bank account.

- More Efficient Payment Systems: CBDCs can provide faster, cheaper, and more efficient payment systems for emerging economies. This can help reduce the cost and time of cross-border transactions, which is particularly important for small businesses and individuals who rely on remittances.

- Enhanced Monetary Policy: CBDCs can provide central banks with better control over monetary policy. By having a direct link to the central bank's monetary policy, CBDCs can provide a more effective tool for implementing and adjusting monetary policy.

Challenges:

- Technical Infrastructure: Emerging economies may not have the necessary technical infrastructure to support the implementation of CBDCs. The digital infrastructure may need significant investment to ensure that CBDCs can be accessed and utilized by all populations.

- Financial Stability: CBDCs could potentially destabilize the financial system of emerging economies. They could lead to a shift in the balance of power between commercial banks and central banks, potentially affecting the stability of the banking sector.

- Regulatory Frameworks: Emerging economies may need to establish regulatory frameworks to ensure the proper use and governance of CBDCs. This includes issues such as cybersecurity[9], privacy, and money laundering.

- Costs and Funding: The development and implementation of CBDCs could require significant investment and funding, which may be a challenge for emerging economies with limited resources.

- Exchange Rate Fluctuations: Emerging economies could face exchange rate fluctuations if their CBDCs become more widely adopted internationally. These fluctuations could impact their trade and economic stability.

Overall, the adoption of CBDCs in emerging economies can offer several benefits, including increased financial inclusion, more efficient payment systems, and enhanced monetary policy. However, these benefits must be weighed against the potential challenges, including the need for technical infrastructure, regulatory frameworks, and funding. CBDCs represent a significant shift in the financial landscape and will require careful consideration and planning for emerging economies.

---

9 Cybersecurity refers to the practices, technologies, and measures used to protect computers, networks, data, and other digital assets from unauthorized access, use, theft, damage, or other forms of cyber threats.

Chapter 30: Opportunities and challenges for advanced economies

Central Bank Digital Currencies (CBDCs) are attracting significant attention from policymakers and financial institutions around the world. Advanced economies, such as the United States, the European Union, and Japan, have been exploring the potential benefits and challenges of CBDCs. In this chapter, we will discuss the opportunities and challenges that advanced economies may face in implementing CBDCs.

Opportunities for Advanced Economies:

- Enhancing Financial Stability: CBDCs can contribute to the stability of the financial system by reducing the risk of bank runs and increasing the effectiveness of monetary policy. In times of crisis, central banks can use CBDCs to provide liquidity to the economy quickly and efficiently.

- Improving Payment Systems: Advanced economies can leverage CBDCs to improve their payment systems, making them faster, cheaper, and more secure. CBDCs can also help reduce the reliance on cash, which can improve financial inclusion and reduce the underground economy.

- Supporting Innovation: CBDCs can support innovation in the financial industry by providing a platform for new payment systems and financial products. CBDCs can also provide a better understanding of how digital currencies work and their potential impact on the economy.

- Strengthening Monetary Policy: CBDCs can help central banks to implement their monetary policy more effectively. CBDCs can provide more accurate and real-time data on the economy, allowing central banks to make better-informed decisions.

Challenges for Advanced Economies:

- Implementation and Adoption: Implementing CBDCs requires significant investment in technology and infrastructure. Advanced economies may also face challenges in adopting CBDCs due to concerns about security, privacy, and regulatory issues.

- Disruption to the Financial System: CBDCs have the potential to disrupt the existing financial system, especially the banking system. Banks could face a reduction in their deposit base, leading to a decrease in lending capacity.

- Cross-Border Transactions: CBDCs may face significant challenges in cross-border transactions, such as interoperability issues, regulatory differences, and political conflicts.

- Privacy Concerns: CBDCs raise concerns about the privacy of individuals' financial transactions. Advanced economies will need to develop privacy-focused regulations to address these concerns.

Conclusion:

The adoption of CBDCs is a complex and challenging task for advanced economies. However, the potential benefits of CBDCs, such as enhancing financial stability, improving payment systems, supporting innovation, and strengthening monetary policy, are significant. To address the challenges of CBDCs, advanced economies will need to develop a comprehensive regulatory framework, invest in technology and infrastructure, and foster international cooperation and coordination.

Chapter 31: Technological advancements and innovation

The development and implementation of CBDCs rely heavily on technological advancements and innovation. In this chapter, we will explore the technological advancements and innovations that are shaping the future of CBDC. In this chapter, we will explore the technological advancements and innovations that are shaping the future of CBDC.

Blockchain Technology

One of the key technological advancements that have enabled the development of CBDCs is blockchain technology. Blockchain is a decentralized and distributed digital ledger that allows for secure and transparent transactions without the need for intermediaries such as banks or other financial institutions. This technology is already being used in various cryptocurrencies such as Bitcoin[10], Ethereum[11], and others.

CBDCs can leverage blockchain technology to enable fast, secure, and low-cost transactions while ensuring transparency and immutability. The use of blockchain technology can also reduce the risk of fraud and counterfeiting, as transactions are validated and recorded in real-time.

---

10 Bitcoin is a digital currency that was created in 2009 by an unknown person or group using the pseudonym Satoshi Nakamoto. Bitcoin is a decentralized currency, which means it is not controlled by any central authority, such as a government or financial institution. Bitcoin operates on a distributed ledger called the blockchain, which maintains a record of all Bitcoin transactions.

11 Ethereum is an open-source, blockchain-based platform that allows developers to build and deploy decentralized applications (DApps) and smart contracts. Ethereum was created in 2015 by Vitalik Buterin, who sought to create a platform that would allow for more complex programmable transactions than Bitcoin.

Smart Contracts

Smart contracts are self-executing computer programs that can automatically execute the terms of a contract when predefined conditions are met. They enable the automation of various processes and eliminate the need for intermediaries such as lawyers or other third parties.

CBDCs can leverage smart contracts to automate various financial transactions such as payments, loans, and other financial agreements. This can reduce the cost and time associated with traditional financial transactions while also increasing security and transparency.

Artificial Intelligence (AI)[12]

Artificial intelligence is another technology that can enable the development of more sophisticated CBDCs. AI can be used to analyze large amounts of data, identify patterns and trends, and make predictions based on historical data. This technology can also be used to develop algorithms that can automate various financial processes such as fraud detection and risk assessment.

CBDCs can leverage AI to enable more efficient and effective financial transactions while reducing the risk of fraud and errors. For example, AI can be used to detect and prevent money laundering by analyzing transaction patterns and identifying suspicious activities.

Internet of Things (IoT)[13]

The Internet of Things is a network of connected devices that can communicate with each other and exchange data. These devices can include smartphones, tablets, wearables, and other smart devices.

---

12 Artificial intelligence (AI) refers to the development of computer systems that can perform tasks that typically require human, such as visual perception, speech intelligence recognition, decision-making, and language translation. AI is achieved through machine learning, where algorithms are trained on large amounts of data and can improve their performance over time. AI can be applied in a wide range of industries, including healthcare, finance, transportation, and manufacturing, and has the potential to revolutionize how we live and work.

CBDCs can leverage IoT to enable seamless and convenient financial transactions. For example, a smartwatch can be used to make a payment by simply tapping it on a payment terminal. This can reduce the need for physical cash or credit cards while also providing a more convenient and secure payment method.

Conclusion

The development and implementation of CBDCs rely heavily on technological advancements and innovation. Blockchain technology, smart contracts, artificial intelligence, and the Internet of Things are just a few examples of the technologies that can enable the development of more efficient, secure, and transparent CBDCs. These technologies can also provide new opportunities and challenges for emerging and advanced economies, as well as the global financial system as a whole. It will be important for policymakers, regulators, and other stakeholders to continue to monitor and adapt to these technological advancements to ensure the safe and efficient use of CBDCs.

---

13 The Internet of Things (IoT) refers to the network of physical devices, vehicles, home appliances, and other items embedded with sensors, software, and connectivity, which enable them to connect and exchange data. IoT devices can communicate with each other and with other systems over the internet, enabling a wide range of applications and services, including home automation, smart cities, industrial automation, and healthcare monitoring.

IX. Fears

Chapter 32: Common people's fears about CBDC

Central Bank Digital Currency (CBDC) has been a topic of discussion in the financial world for some time now. While CBDC has the potential to bring many benefits to the economy and society, some people still have concerns about its implementation. In this chapter, we will explore some common people's fears about CBDC.

- Privacy concerns: One of the biggest fears about CBDC is privacy. Since transactions made with CBDC are recorded on a public ledger, there is a fear that this information could be used by governments or other entities to monitor individuals' financial transactions. Some people worry that their financial information could be used against them.

- Cybersecurity risks: CBDC is a digital currency, which means that it is susceptible to cyber attacks. Many people fear that if CBDC is hacked, their financial information could be stolen, and they could lose their money. This fear is especially prevalent among older individuals who may not be as familiar with digital technology.

- Potential for inflation: There is a fear that the introduction of CBDC could lead to inflation. Since CBDC is backed by the central bank, some people worry that the government could print too much of it, leading to a decrease in the currency's value.

- Lack of anonymity: Some people fear that CBDC will eliminate anonymity in financial transactions. While some people may appreciate the transparency of public ledgers, others fear that their financial transactions could be traced back to them, compromising their privacy.

- Dependence on technology: CBDC is a digital currency, which means that it requires access to technology to use. Some people worry that this could create a digital divide, where those who do not have access to technology are left behind. Additionally, there is a fear that if the technology fails, individuals could lose access to their funds.

- Potential for government overreach: CBDC is issued by the central bank, which means that the government has a lot of control over its use. Some people worry that this could lead to government overreach, where the government could use CBDC to control individuals' financial transactions.

Chapter 33: Business concerns about CBDC

Central Bank Digital Currency (CBDC) is a new form of digital currency issued by a central bank that has the potential to transform the financial landscape. While CBDC offers several benefits, it also poses certain challenges and concerns, especially for businesses.

Here are some of the main business concerns about CBDC:

- Disruption of business models: CBDC can potentially disrupt traditional business models by reducing the need for intermediaries in financial transactions. This could impact financial institutions, payment providers, and other intermediaries that facilitate transactions between businesses and consumers. As a result, some businesses may need to re-evaluate their business models and adapt to the changing landscape.

- Cybersecurity risks: With the increasing use of digital currencies, there is a growing concern about cybersecurity risks. CBDC could become a target for cybercriminals who could steal or manipulate digital assets. Businesses that hold CBDC may need to invest in robust cybersecurity measures to protect their assets from potential cyber threats.

- Impact on financial stability: CBDC could impact financial stability by changing the dynamics of the financial system. For instance, if CBDC gains widespread adoption, it could lead to a reduction in bank deposits and a shift in the balance of power between banks and central banks. This could potentially affect the availability of credit and liquidity in the financial system.

- Operational challenges: Implementing CBDC can be challenging and costly for businesses. They may need to invest in new infrastructure and technology to enable CBDC transactions. This could pose a challenge for smaller businesses that may not have the necessary resources to invest in the new technology.

- Legal and regulatory uncertainty: There is still some legal and regulatory uncertainty around CBDC, especially in terms of taxation and anti-money laundering (AML[14]) and know-your-customer (KYC[15]) requirements. Businesses that hold CBDC may need to navigate through a complex regulatory landscape and comply with various regulations.

In conclusion, CBDC offers several benefits for businesses, including faster and cheaper transactions, increased financial inclusion, and reduced transaction costs. However, it also poses certain challenges and concerns, especially for businesses that may need to adapt to the changing financial landscape. It is important for businesses to carefully evaluate the potential risks and benefits of CBDC and develop strategies to manage the risks and take advantage of the opportunities presented by this new technology.

---

14 AML stands for Anti-Money Laundering, which refers to the laws, regulations, and procedures implemented by governments and financial institutions to prevent, detect, and report activities that involve the concealment of illegally obtained funds or assets. Money laundering is the process by which criminals try to make their illegally obtained money appear legitimate, usually by using a series of transactions or investments to hide the source of the funds. AML regulations aim to prevent this by requiring financial institutions to conduct due diligence on their customers, monitor transactions for suspicious activity, and report any suspicious transactions or behavior to the appropriate authorities. The goal of AML is to prevent the use of the financial system for illicit activities and to protect the integrity of the financial system as a whole.

15 KYC stands for Know Your Customer, which refers to the process by which businesses verify the identity of their clients or customers. The purpose of KYC is to prevent identity theft, fraud, money laundering, and other illegal activities by ensuring that customers are who they claim to be. KYC typically involves collecting and verifying personal information such as name, address, date of birth, and government-issued identification documents. This information is used to assess the customer's risk profile and determine the level of due diligence required. KYC regulations are commonly found in the financial services industry, but are also used in other sectors such as telecommunications, gaming, and e-commerce.

Chapter 34: State concerns about CBDC

While CBDCs have many potential benefits, governments and central banks are also considering the potential challenges that may arise from their implementation. Some of the state concerns regarding CBDCs are:

- Monetary policy control: One of the primary concerns of central banks is the potential impact of CBDCs on their ability to control monetary policy. Since CBDCs can provide a direct channel for the central bank to distribute money, it could create challenges in controlling the money supply and managing inflation. Central banks need to ensure that they have the necessary tools to maintain monetary stability while also ensuring the successful implementation of CBDCs.

- Financial stability: Another concern for central banks is the impact of CBDCs on financial stability. Since CBDCs would provide an alternative to traditional bank deposits, it could lead to a significant shift in the structure of the financial system. Central banks must ensure that the implementation of CBDCs does not destabilize the financial system and that it complements the existing financial infrastructure.

- Cybersecurity and operational risks: Central banks also need to consider the potential cybersecurity and operational risks associated with CBDCs. Since CBDCs would rely on digital infrastructure, it is vulnerable to cyber attacks, hacking, and other types of operational failures. Central banks must ensure that the necessary measures are in place to mitigate these risks and protect the financial system from potential threats.

- Privacy and surveillance concerns: Governments must consider the privacy and surveillance implications of CBDCs. While CBDCs can provide increased transparency and accountability, it can also lead to concerns about government surveillance and invasion of privacy. It is essential to balance the need for transparency with the right to privacy and ensure that adequate measures are in place to protect individuals' personal information.

- Legal and regulatory frameworks: Governments need to establish clear legal and regulatory frameworks for the implementation and operation of CBDCs. Since CBDCs represent a significant shift in the financial system, it requires new regulations and legal structures to govern its use. Governments must work to develop clear guidelines and frameworks to ensure that CBDCs are safe, secure, and effective for users.

In summary, CBDCs offer many potential benefits, but their implementation also presents challenges that must be carefully considered. Central banks and governments need to work together to develop appropriate legal, regulatory, and technological infrastructure to ensure the successful implementation of CBDCs.

X. Conclusion

Chapter 35: Recap of key points

In conclusion, Central Bank Digital Currency (CBDC) is a digital form of currency issued and backed by a central bank. It is a new concept in the financial world that is gaining popularity due to its potential to revolutionize the way we use and access money.

One of the primary advantages of CBDC is increased financial inclusion, as it provides an easy and accessible means for unbanked and underbanked individuals to participate in the financial system. It also has the potential to reduce fraud and corruption, enhance monetary policy, and increase the efficiency of payment systems.

However, there are also several challenges and disadvantages associated with CBDC, including the potential threat to commercial banks, privacy concerns, operational and technical challenges, and risks of centralization.

CBDC can be compared with other payment systems, such as cash, traditional electronic payment systems, and cryptocurrencies, and has been implemented in several countries, including China, Sweden, Uruguay, the Bahamas, Nigeria, Jamaica, South Korea, and France.

Regulatory issues and challenges surrounding CBDC include legal and regulatory frameworks, cross-border transactions and interoperability, and international cooperation and coordination.

The future of CBDC is promising, with potential impacts on the global financial system, opportunities and challenges for both advanced and emerging economies, and technological advancements and innovation driving its development.

In summary, CBDC has the potential to transform the financial industry, but it is essential to address the challenges and issues associated with its implementation carefully. A collaborative and coordinated approach between regulators, central banks, and other stakeholders will be crucial in realizing the full potential of CBDC.

Chapter 36: Implications for policymakers, financial institutions, and consumers

The introduction of Central Bank Digital Currency (CBDC) has the potential to significantly impact policymakers, financial institutions, and consumers. In this chapter, we will discuss the implications for each of these groups.

For policymakers, CBDC presents an opportunity to increase financial inclusion and enhance monetary policy effectiveness. However, policymakers must also address regulatory and legal issues surrounding CBDC, including privacy concerns, cross-border transactions, and international coordination.

For financial institutions, CBDC presents both opportunities and challenges. On the one hand, CBDC could provide a new revenue stream and reduce transaction costs. On the other hand, CBDC could pose a threat to the traditional banking system, particularly if consumers switch from bank deposits to CBDC.

For consumers, CBDC could offer benefits such as increased financial inclusion and lower transaction costs. However, consumers may also face privacy concerns, and the adoption of CBDC may require significant changes in how they conduct financial transactions.

Overall, the implications of CBDC for policymakers, financial institutions, and consumers will depend on the specific design and implementation of CBDC. Policymakers must balance the benefits of CBDC with the potential risks and challenges, while financial institutions must adapt to new technological advancements and innovate to remain competitive. Consumers must also weigh the benefits and risks of CBDC adoption and adjust their financial behaviors accordingly.

In conclusion, CBDC is a complex and rapidly evolving area of finance that presents significant opportunities and challenges for policymakers, financial institutions, and consumers. The successful implementation and adoption of CBDC will require careful consideration of these implications and a willingness to adapt to the changing financial landscape.

Chapter 37: Should you be afraid of CBDC?

Central Bank Digital Currency (CBDC) has been a hot topic of discussion in the world of finance and technology in recent years. CBDCs are digital versions of fiat currencies issued by a central bank and are backed by government guarantees. The implementation of CBDCs could have significant implications for the global financial system and the way we conduct transactions. Some people are worried about the potential consequences of CBDCs, while others believe they will bring about positive changes. In this chapter, we will explore whether you should be afraid of CBDC.

What are the benefits of CBDC?

One of the main advantages of CBDC is its potential to increase financial inclusion. With CBDCs, individuals who don't have access to traditional banking services can participate in the financial system. This could lead to increased economic growth and reduced poverty rates. CBDCs could also reduce transaction costs and increase the speed of payments, making it easier for people to send and receive money across borders.

CBDCs could also help reduce the risks associated with cash transactions, such as counterfeiting and money laundering. Transactions made with CBDCs are transparent, traceable, and cannot be counterfeited, making them more secure than cash. Additionally, CBDCs can be programmed with features such as expiration dates or spending limits to prevent fraud and protect consumers.

What are the potential risks of CBDC?

Despite the potential benefits, there are also some risks associated with CBDCs. One of the main concerns is that CBDCs could lead to increased surveillance and loss of privacy. Since all transactions made with CBDCs are traceable, governments or central banks could potentially monitor people's financial activities. This could lead to violations of privacy and civil liberties. Additionally, CBDCs could create a single point of failure in the financial system, making it vulnerable to cyber attacks.

Another concern is that CBDCs could disrupt the banking system and lead to financial instability. If people start using CBDCs instead of traditional bank accounts, it could lead to a decrease in demand for banks, potentially leading to bank failures and systemic risk. Moreover, if the central bank directly offers digital currency to the public, it could disrupt the commercial banking system by depriving banks of their role as intermediaries.

Should you be afraid of CBDC?

In conclusion, whether or not you should be afraid of CBDCs depends on your perspective. If you are concerned about privacy and government surveillance, you may view CBDCs with suspicion. However, if you are optimistic about the potential for financial inclusion and reducing transaction costs, you may welcome the implementation of CBDCs. Ultimately, the success or failure of CBDCs will depend on how they are implemented and regulated. It is essential to weigh the potential benefits and risks and make informed decisions about whether or not to use CBDCs.

Chapter 38: Final thoughts and recommendations

Throughout this guide, we have examined the advantages and disadvantages of CBDC, as well as the different approaches and case studies of CBDC implementation. We have also discussed the various regulatory challenges that need to be addressed, as well as the potential impact on the global financial system and the opportunities and challenges for emerging and advanced economies.

Overall, CBDC has the potential to revolutionize the way we conduct financial transactions. It could increase financial inclusion, reduce fraud and corruption, enhance monetary policy, and provide a more efficient and secure payment system. However, there are also potential disadvantages such as the risks of centralization, privacy concerns, operational and technical challenges, and the threat to commercial banks.

For policymakers, CBDC presents an opportunity to improve financial inclusion and enhance monetary policy. However, policymakers also need to ensure that the regulatory framework is in place to address potential risks and ensure that CBDC operates in a safe and secure manner.

For financial institutions, CBDC presents both opportunities and challenges. On the one hand, it could lead to greater efficiency and cost savings. On the other hand, it could also threaten the role of commercial banks in the financial system.

For consumers, CBDC could provide a more secure and efficient payment system, but also raises concerns about privacy and surveillance.

Therefore, it is essential for policymakers, financial institutions, and consumers to carefully consider the implications of CBDC and work together to develop a framework that addresses potential risks while maximizing the benefits. Collaboration among countries and international organizations is also necessary to address cross-border interoperability issues and ensure that CBDC operates seamlessly across different jurisdictions.

XI. References

1. BIS (2018). "Central Bank Digital Currencies." Bank for International Settlements.

2. Yermack, D. (2015). "Is Bitcoin a Real Currency?" National Bureau of Economic Research.

3. Huang, J., & Zhou, Z. (2019). "Central Bank Digital Currency and Its Economic Implications." Economic Perspectives.

4. World Bank (2020). "Central Bank Digital Currencies: Opportunities, Risks and Challenges." World Bank Group.

5. McKinsey & Company (2019). "Central Bank Digital Currencies: A New Era of Digital Money." McKinsey & Company.

6. ECB (2020). "Report on a Digital Euro." European Central Bank.

7. G20 (2019). "G20 High-level Principles for Digital Financial Inclusion." G20 Osaka Summit.

8. BIS (2021). "Central Bank Digital Currencies: Foundational Principles and Core Features." Bank for International Settlements.

9. IMF (2021). "Legal Aspects of Central Bank Digital Currencies." International Monetary Fund.

10. Bank of Canada (2020). "Central Bank Digital Currency: Motivations and Implications." Bank of Canada.

11. BIS. (2021). Central bank digital currencies: foundational principles and core features.

12. Deutsche Bank Research. (2021). CBDCs: A new era of central banking?

13. Eichengreen, B., & Shin, H. S. (2021). Central bank digital currency: The quest for minimally invasive technology. Journal of Economic Perspectives, 35(1), 3-24.

14. Engert, W., Hendry, S., & Moran, C. (2021). Central bank digital currencies: foundational principles and core features. Bank of Canada.

15. Federal Reserve Board. (2021). Central bank digital currencies: A literature review.

16. IMF. (2021). Central bank digital currencies: Opportunities, risks and challenges.

17. World Economic Forum. (2020). Central bank digital currencies: Central banking for the digital age.

18. Bank for International Settlements. (2020). Central bank digital currencies. BIS Papers, No. 107.

19. Bank of Canada. (2021). Central bank digital currency: Opportunities, challenges and design. Discussion paper.

20. Bank of England. (2020). Central bank digital currency: opportunities, challenges and design. Discussion paper.

21. Barontini, C., & Holden, H. (2020). Proceeding with caution-a survey on central bank digital currency. BIS Quarterly Review, September.

22. Carstens, A. (2018). Central bank digital currencies. Speech at the Hoover Institution, Stanford University.

23. European Central Bank. (2021). Report on a digital euro.

24. FSB. (2020). Enhancing cross-border payments: Stage 3 roadmap.

25. Goodhart, C., & Jensen, M. (2021). Central bank digital currencies and banking. Journal of Banking Regulation, 22(2), 83-97.

26. Mancini-Griffoli, T., et al. (2021). Digital currencies: the rise of stablecoins. IMF Discussion Note, No. 21/02.

27. Nakamoto, S. (2008). Bitcoin: A peer-to-peer electronic cash system.

28. Raskin, M., & Yermack, D. (2016). Digital currencies, decentralized ledgers, and the future of central banking. Annual Review of Financial Economics, 8, 397-416.

29. Sveriges Riksbank. (2020). The e-krona project. First interim report.

30. U.S. Federal Reserve. (2021). Federal Reserve Board announces launch of the central bank digital currency (CBDC) research project.

31. World Bank. (2021). The Global Findex Database 2017: Measuring Financial Inclusion and the Fintech Revolution.

32. Central Bank Digital Currency: Opportunities, Challenges, and Design by Raphael Auer, Giulio Cornelli, Jon Frost, and Henry Holden (2020).

33. Central Bank Digital Currency and Fintech in Asia by Douglas W. Arner, Paul P. S. Lai, and Wilson Chow (2021)

34. Central Bank Digital Currency: The End of Monetary Policy As We Know It? by Dirk Niepelt (2020)

35. Digital Currencies and Stablecoins: Policy, Risks, and Potential by Dong He (2020)

36. The Handbook of Digital Currency: Bitcoin, Innovation, Financial Instruments, and Big Data edited by David Lee Kuo Chuen and Robert Deng (2015)

37. Cryptocurrency, Blockchain, and Bitcoin: A Guide for Accounting and Business Professionals by Sean Stein Smith (2020)

38. Handbook of Blockchain, Digital Finance, and Inclusion, Volume 1: Cryptocurrency, FinTech, InsurTech, and Regulation edited by David Lee Kuo Chuen and Robert H. Deng (2019)

39. World Economic Forum. (2020). Central Bank Digital Currency Policy-Maker Toolkit.

40. World Economic Forum. (2022). Nineteen countries in the G20 - which represents the world's largest economies - are exploring central bank digital currencies, including Japan, India, Russia and South Korea. As mentioned above, the US and UK are researching CBDCs, but have not yet committed to introducing them.

41. The Economist. (2022). According to the Atlantic Council, a think-tank in Washington, DC, 89 countries making up 90% of world GDP are exploring a CBDC. The Bahamian sand dollar, the East Caribbean D Cash and...

42. IMF. (2022). We know that the move towards CBDCs is gaining momentum, driven by the ingenuity of Central Banks. All told, around 100 countries are exploring CBDCs at one level or another. Some researching, some testing, and a few already distributing CBDC to the public. In the Bahamas, the Sand Dollar—the local CBDC—has been in circulation for more than a year.

43. Ozili, Peterson K. (2022). Central bank digital currency research around the World: a review of literature.

44. The World Bank. (2022). ECA Talk: Digital Currencies and the Challenges for Central Banks.

45. Finextra. (2022). CBDCs: Here's what every central bank in the world is working on.

46. CBDC Tracker - https://cbdctracker.org